Mr. Flu Go Away

Written by Dave Thomas

Illustrated by Mike Motz

Mr. Flu Go Away

Written by Dave Thomas

Illustrated by Mike Motz

In the wintertime,
it gets really cold. Brrr.

SLEDDING HILL

SCHOOL

Sometimes I get sick because of
how cold it is outside.

My mom says that germs
make me get sick too.

Be Kind to A
EDWINA

One of the germs that
makes me sick is Mr. Flu.

When he comes,
I get really sick.

I get a fever that makes
me really hot and tired.

Mom has to give me medicine
to make it go away. Sometimes
the medicine tastes yummy.

Be Kind to Animals

But sometimes it doesn't.
Yuck!!!

When Mr. Flu comes, I
sneeze and cough a lot too.
Achoo!!!

AH-
CHOO!

HONK!

I have a runny nose all the time.
I have to use a lot of tissues.

Sometimes it's hard to breathe
because my nose is stuffy,
and I can't sleep.

Mommy rubs something smelly
on my neck and chest to help
me breathe better so I can
get some rest.

Mr. Flu makes me so sick that I can't go to school for a few days. I miss my teacher, friends, and recess.

After a few days, I usually wake up feeling a lot better. I have a lot of energy, and I'm ready to go back to school. Mr. Flu finally went away.

My mom and dad are really
happy that I feel better.

About the Author

David Thomas is an African American poet and author who is new to the children's book genre. He was born and raised in Brooklyn, NY, and now lives in Queens, NY, with his beautiful wife and three boys. He brings a fresh perspective and unique style of storytelling in his writing that really connects with young readers. In this book, he once again showcases his amazing ability to take complex concepts and explain them to young children.

You can connect with him, find out about his upcoming books, and check out his poetry on Instagram @poeticflames.